INSTANT
Yiddish

by
Fred Kogos

A CITADEL PRESS BOOK
Published by Carol Publishing Group

Carol Publishing Group Edition, 1995

A Citadel Press Book
Published by Carol Publishing Group
Citadel Press is a registered trademark of Carol Communications, Inc.

Editorial Offices: 600 Madison Avenue, New York, NY 10022
Sales & Distribution Offices: 120 Enterprise Avenue, Secaucus, NJ 07094
In Canada: Canadian Manda Group, One Atlantic Avenue, Suite 105
Toronto, Ontario, M6K 3E7

Queries regarding rights and permissions should be addressed to:
Carol Publishing Group, 600 Madison Avenue, New York, NY 10022

Manufactured in the United States of America
ISBN 0-8065-1154-0

15   14   13   12   11   10   9

Carol Publishing Group books are available at special discounts
for bulk purchases, sales promotions, fund raising, or
educational purposes. Special editions can also be created to
specifications. For details contact: Special Sales Department,
Carol Publishing Group, 120 Enterprise Ave., Secaucus, NJ 07094

CONTENTS

Introduction

There's such a fuss these days about being Jewish and bicultural that it is considered quite "in" to be bilingual and speak Yiddish, or at least know some Yiddishisms—words, phrases, or expressions —and how to use them.

If you grew up in a Yiddish-speaking home, you learned some of the language. If you grew up on the lower East Side of New York, or in any other Jewish quarter in the U.S.A., you had a golden opportunity to learn Yiddish casually. If you did not have this opportunity earlier in your life, but wish to get on the Yiddish bandwagon, without having to go to school, then presto! *Instant Yiddish* is for you!

This booklet was written primarily for those who are completely unfamiliar with Yiddish pronunciation. It is also a splendid refresher course for those who once knew Yiddish but have forgotten it.

The Yiddish words in this book have been transliterated phonetically into the Roman alphabet, so it will be quite easy for you to speak Yiddish instantly and make friends or influence sales or put some variety in your conversation.

This booklet will enable you to get along and make yourself understood anywhere in the world where Yiddish is spoken. And that means practically everywhere!

FACTS ABOUT YIDDISH

Yiddish is spoken by about 10,000,000 people throughout the world. In Russia, Poland, Rumania, England, France and other European countries, in the United States and Canada, Israel, Africa, Latin America, New Zealand, Australia, and wherever else East European Jews migrated, Yiddish survives as a spoken language—in the home, on the streets, in the theatre, literature, newspapers and the entertainment field. There is at this moment a strong revival of Yiddish throughout the United States.

Yiddish, whose principal parent is Middle High German, is also related directly to English, Hebrew, Russian, and Polish. And since its birth, in about the year 1100, it has borrowed from other languages as well.

There are four principal accents in Yiddish: Lithuanian, Ukrainian (Galician), Polish, and German (from which come "Litvak," "Galitsianer," and other regional nicknames for Jews). The essential difference between the four lies in the pronunciation—whether it is long or short. We have the same difference in this country, between northern, sourthern, New England, western, and New York accents—each having easily distinguishable characteristics. And still we all understand each other.

In *Instant Yiddish* a standard form is used, one which is based on the usage of the majority and which is understood by any Yiddish-speaking group.

YOU ALREADY KNOW LOTS OF YIDDISH

Since *Yiddish* is derived largely from Middle High
German, which relates to the Saxon part of Anglo-
Saxon, many English words are similar to their
Yiddish counterparts. Also we have many cognate words whose roots in both English and Yiddish are alike. Only their pronunciation makes
it difficult to recognize them. But their presence
will be a great help to you when you speak Yiddish. And humorously enough, if you deliberately
mispronounce such cognate words in a broken
English, they usually come out as perfect Yiddish.
Here are a few: *vinter* (winter), *zinger* (singer),
zumer (summer), *hand* (hand), *gut* (good) *epl*
(apple), *broyt* (bread), *orem* (arm), *bahken*
(bake), *bod* (bath), *bord* (beard), *beis* (bite),
bruder (brother), *breng* (bring), *hoys* (house),
putter (butter), *kalt* (cold), *kiel* (cool), *kuzineh*
(cousin), *tochter* (daughter), *zun* (son), *fahl*
(fall) and many others, including numbers.

Besides the words which closely resemble English, there are other Yiddish words (about 500),
which, in their original form, have become part
of our everyday language and are even found in
Webster's Third International Dictionary. Among
them are: *gezundheit* (good health, bless you!),
kindergarten (kindergarten), *shlemiel* (clumsy
dope), *shlimazel* (unlucky person), *mazel* (luck),
shmo (patsy), *kibbitz* (to meddle), *shikker*
(drunkard), *shalom* (peace, hello), *tzimmes*
(fruit compote; in slang "big deal"), *bar mitzvah*
(confirmation), *gefilte fish* (stuffed fish), *halvah*
(candy made of crushed sesame seeds and honey),
kosher (proper Jewish food, OK!), mitzvah
(comandment, good deed), *bris* (circumcision),
shnook (a dolt), and many others.

ADVICE ABOUT PRONUNCIATION

Vowels	Diphthongs	Consonants
a as in father	**ai** as in say or	**dz** as in sounds
i as in lit	main	**g** as in go
e as in bed	**ei** as in by or	**ch** as in loch
o as in hot	height	or Bach
u as in put	**oi** or **oy** as in	**r** soft (no trill)
	boy or voice	**ts** as in pats
	(When two other	**tsh** or **tch** as in
	vowels appear to-	church
	gether, pronounce	**zh** as in seizure
	them separately.)	

AS TO ACCENT

In words of two syllables, the accent usually falls on the first syllable. In words of three syllables or more, the accent usually falls on the second syllable. Words elongated by prefixes or suffixes retain the original accent. (I hope that is not too *onge-patchket* [muddled] for you!)

SPECIAL NOTES ON ACCENTS AND PRONUNCIATION

ahf and oyf   There are a number of words, diphthongs, and phonemes whose spellings represent the pronunciations of their locale—Russian, Polish, German, etc. Sometimes the same word has two phonetic appearances, for example, *ahf* and *oyf*. As the author heard or himself used them, so he recorded them here. Although every effort was made for internal consistency throughout this work, the author felt compelled to retain the pronunciations which sounded most natural to his ear. The attuned ear will appreciate this, although the educated eye would prefer *oyf* to *ahf*.

"h" after the vowel   In many cases the letter h appears after the vowel, as in *ahf* (on), *bohmer* (bum), and so on. The purpose of this is to

broaden the vowel. If you pronounce the "a" in _ahf_ as in "after," you're wrong! _Ahf_ must rhyme with the "a" as in "father."

"h" at the end of the word   The letter "h" has been added to many words that end in vowels to make sure that the vowel is pronounced as a separate syllable.

HOW TO USE THIS PHRASE BOOK

This guide is easy to use. It is divided according to situations you are likely to be in. Each expression is in transliterated Yiddish, and all you have to do is pronounce it as it is written.

The words and phrases included represent the most-used expressions, those which most often appear in guide books published by private firms, travel and airline companies and the U.S. War Department. Organized in short sentences and words which are easy to repeat and remember, this booklet will prepare you for everyday life experiences with expressions that are constantly used by people speaking to you, so that you will be able to understand them and be understood by them in turn. And this holds true not only for the U.S.A. but abroad as well.

Yiddish is becoming so universal these days that knowing a little of it will facilitate daily contacts with Jews in your travels at home and abroad, help you in emergencies, make friends for you and give you altogether a pleasant feeling and a fascinating adventure. _Fort • gezunterhait_ (bon voyage) and _sholom alaichem_ (peace be unto you). And above all _mazel tov!_ (good luck to you!).

ONE _____

Words
and Phrases
Classified

Remember the pronunciations: A=ah; Ai=ay; E=eh; Ei=i; I=ee (or i as in it); O as in toss; U as in put; Ch as in Scottish "loch" or German "lach"; Oi and Oy, S and Z, Nit and Nisht, Oo and U, and Ahf and Oyf are used interchangeably

WHEN YOU MEET PEOPLE

Yes yoh

No nain

Good gut

Thank you. A dank.

Glad to meet you. Tsufriden eich tsu kenen.

You are welcome. Nit do far vos.

Excuse me. Zeit moichel; antshuldik mir.

It's all right. Es iz gants gut.

Please. Zeit azoy gut.

I would like ich volt velen

What? Vos?

This dos

Where vu

Here doh

When ven

Now itzt

Later shpeter

Who ver

I ich

You du (sing.), ir (pl.)

He er

She zi

Your name? Eier nomen? Vi haist ir?

My name is... Ich hais...

Good morning. Gut morgen.

Good evening. Gutn ovent.

Good night. A gute nacht.

Good-by. A gutn. Shalom.

How are you? Vos macht ir?

Very well, thank you, and you? Zaier gut, a dank, un vos macht ir?

I do not understand. Please repeat. Ich farshtai nit. Zeit azoy gut, chazert es iber.

So long. Zeit gezunt.

See you again. Me vet zich zen.

I'm sorry. Es tut mir laid.

WHEN YOU NEED NUMBERS

Cardinal Numbers

One ains
Two tsvai
Three drei
Four fir
Five finf
Six zeks
Seven ziben
Eight acht
Nine nein
Ten tsen
Eleven elef
Twelve tsvelf

Thirteen   dreitsen
Fourteen   fertsen
Fifteen   fuftsen
Sixteen   zechtsen
Seventeen   zibetsen
Eighteen   achtsen
Nineteen   neintsen
Twenty   tsvontsik
Twenty-one   ain-un tsvontsik
Thirty   dreisik
Forty   fertsik
Fifty   fuftsik
Sixty   zechtsik
Seventy   zibetsik
Eighty   achtsik
Niuety   neintsik
One hundred   hundert
Thousand   toyzent
Million   milyon

Ordinal Numbers

First   ershte(r)
Second   tsvaite(r)
Third   dritte(r)
Fourth   ferte(r)
Fifth   finfte(r)
Sixth   zekste(r)
Seventh   zibete(r)
Eighth   achte(r)
Ninth   neinte(r)
Tenth   tsente(r)
Eleventh   elfte(r)
Twelfth   tsvelfte(r)

WHEN YOU GO TO A HOTEL

Where is a good hotel?   Vu iz a guter hotel?
I want a room.   Ich vil a tsimmer.
  For one person.   Oif ain mentsch.
  For two persons.   Oif tsvai mentschen.
  With bath.   Mit a vanneh.
  For two days.   Far tsvai teg.
  For a week.   Far a voch.

Till Monday. Biz montik.
  Tuesday. dinstik.
  Wednesday. mitvoch.
  Thursday. donershtik.
  Friday. freitik.
  Saturday. shabbes.
  Sunday. zuntik.

How much is it? Vifil kost es?

Here is my passport. Ot iz mein pass.

Here are my bags. Ot iz mein bagazh.

I like it. Es gefelt mir.

I don't like it. Es gefelt mir nit.

Show me anotner room. Veist mir an ander tsimmer.

Where is the toilet? Vu iz der klozet?

Where is the men's room? Vu iz dos vashtsimmer
  far menner?

Where is the ladies' room? Vu iz dos vashtsimmer
  far froien?

Hot water haiseh vasser

A towel a hantech

Soap zaif

Come in! Kumt arein!

Please, I want to have this washed. Zeit azoy gut, ich
  vil lozen dos oysvashen.
  Press, v. oyspressen
  Clean, v. oysrainiken

When will it be ready? Ven vet es zein fartig?

I need it for tonight. Ich darf es oyf heint ovnt.
  for tomorrow. Oyf morgen.

Put it there. Laig es dorten.

My key, please. Mein shlisel, zeit azoy gut.

Any mail for me? Iz doh far mir a briv?

Any packages? Zeinen doh packlech?

I want five airmail stamps for the United States. Ich vil
  finf luftpost markes far di farainikteh shtaten.

I want to send a telegram. Ich vil shiken a telegrameh.

Some postcards etlechch postkartlech

Call me at seven in the morning. Ruft mir ziben a zaiger in der fri.

Where is the telephone? Vu iz der telefon?

Hello! Haloh! Shalom!

Send breakfast to room 702, please. Shikt arein frishtik tsum tsimmer ziben hundert un tsvai, zeit azoy gut.

Orange juice marantsn-zaft

Rolls and coffee bulkes un kaveh

I am expecting someone. Ich dervart emetsen.

Tell him (her) to wait for me. Zog im (ir) tsu varten oyf mir.

If anyone calls me, I'll be back at six. Oyb emetser telefonirt mir, vel ich tsurik kumen seks a zaiger.

Tell me, please, where is there a drug store? Zogt mir, zeit azoy gut, vu iz doh an apteik?
  a barber shop? a sherer?
  a beauty parlor? a shainkeit salon?

What is the telephone number? Vos iz der telefon-numer?

What is the address? Vos iz der adres?

I want to change some money. Ich vil oysbeiten a bissel gelt.

What is the rate to the dollar? Vifil iz der kurs fun dolar?

My bill, please. Mein cheshben, zeit azoy gut.

WHEN YOU GO TO EAT

I am hungry. Ich bin hungerik.

I'm thirsty. Ich bin durshtik.

I want to eat. Ich vil essen.

Where is a good restaurant? Vu is doh a guter restoran?

A table for two, please. A tish far tsvai, zait azoy gut.

Waiter! Kelner!

Waitress! Kelneren!

The menu, please. Di shpaizkart, zeit azoy gut.

What is good today? Vos iz gut heint?

Is it ready? Es iz fartig?

How long will it take? Vi lang vet es nemen?

This, please. Dos, zeit azoy gut.

Bring some water. Brengt mir a bissel vasser.

A glass of beer a gloz bir

Milk milch

White wine veisser vein

Red wine royter vein

A cocktail a coktail

A whisky soda a viski mit sodeh

To your health! Down the hatch! L'cheiyim!

Soup zup, yoich

Fish fish

Meat flaish

Bread and butter broyt mit putter

A sandwich a sendvich

Roasted chicken gebroteneh hun

Veal cutlets kelberneh kotleten

Beef stew rinderner gulash

Salt and Pepper zalts un feffer

Steak ku-flaish, oksen-flaish

Rare nit derbroten

Well-done gut durchgebroten

I don't want any sauce. Ich vil nit kain gedempts.

With potatoes mit kartofles

Fried gepregelteh

Rice reiz

An omelet a feinkuchen

And what vegetables? Un vossereh grins?

Peas arbes

Carrots meren

Beans beblach, fasolyes

Onions tsibeles

Cauliflower kalafyor

Salads salaten

Lettuce salat

Tomatoes tomaten

Cucumber ugerkeh

Please bring me another fork. Zeit azoy gut, brengt mir an anderen gopel.

Knife messer

Spoon leffel

Glass gloz

Plate teller

What is there for desert? Vos hot ir far kompot?

Fruit frucht

Pastry gebeks

Strawberry trushkaveh

Ice cream eiz krem

Pie flodn

Cheese kez

Cheese cake kez-kuchen

Honey cake honik-lekech

Swiss cheese shvaitser kez

Black coffee, please. Shvartzeh kaveh, zeit azoy gut.

With or without sugar? Mit tzuker oder on tzuker?

Coffee with cream kaveh mit shmant

Tea with lemon tai mit limeneh

Mineral water mineral vasser

A little more, please. A bissel mer, zeit azoy gut.

That's enough. Shoyn genug.

The check, please. Dem cheshben, zeit azoy gut.

Is the tip included? Iz dos trinkgelt areingerechent?

It was very good. Es iz geven zaier gut.

WHEN YOU GO SHOPPING

I would like to buy this. Ich volt gevolt dos koyfen.

And that   un dos

I am just looking around. Ich kuk zich nor arum.

Something cheaper, please. Epes biliger, zeit azoy gut.

It's too much. Ez iz tsu fil.

What do you call this? Vi haist dos?

Where is the department for   Vu is der optail far
   raincoats? regen-mantlen?
   a hat? a hitel?
   men's clothing? menner klaider?
   women's clothing? froyen klaider?
   underwear? untervesh?
   shoes? shich?
   a pair of gloves? a por hentchkes?
   stockings? zoken?
   socks? shkar-peten?
   shirts? hemder?

In America my size is . . . In amerika mein moz iz . . .

Toys shpitseig, shpilchelech, tsatskes

Perfume parfum

Costume jewelry kinstlech tsirung

Watches zaigers

Sport articles sport zachen

Show me. Veist mir.

Another one   an anderer

A better quality   a bessereh kvalitet

Bigger gresser

Smaller klener

I don't like the color. Der kolir gefelt mir nit.

I want that. Ich vil dos.

in green. in grin.
yellow. gel.
blue. bioy.
red. royt.
gray. groy.
white. veis.
black. shvarts.
brown. broyn.
pink. rozeh.
lighter. heler, lichtiker.
darker. tunkeler.

I'll take it with me. Ich vel es nemen mit zich.

Please, have it delivered. Zeit azoy gut, brengt es tsu.

A receipt, please. A kaboleh, zeit azoy gut.

Where is there Vu iz do
   a book store? a bicher-krom?
   department store? universal gesheft?
   a flower shop? a blumen-krom?
   a food store? a shpaiz-krom?

Where can I buy Vu ken ich koyfen
   stamps? markes?
   toothpaste? tson-pasteh?

Sale! Oysfarkoyf!

WHEN YOU GO TRAVELLING

Bon voyage! Fort gezunterhait!

Taxi! Taksi!

Take me to the airport. Firt mich tsum fliplats.

Go slow! Pavolyeh! Pamelech!

Turn right. Farkerevet zich oyf rechts.
Turn left. Farkerevet zich oyf links.

Straight ahead. Fort gleich.

Not so fast! Nit azoy gich!

Stop here! Shtelt zich op doh!

How much is it to . . .? Vifil kost es tsu . . .?
And back? Un tsurik?

How-much by the hour?   Vifil kost a sho?
   by the day?   a tog?

What is that building?   Vos iz der binyen?
Can it be visited?   Meh ken es bazuchen?

I want to see the . . .   Ich vil zaien di . . .

To the railroad station.   Tsu der ban-stantsyeh.
   Tsum vagzal.

Wait for me.   Vart oyf mir.

Porter!   Treger!

A ticket to . . .   a bilet tsu . . .

I have two bags.   Ich hob tsvai valizes.

One way   ain richtung

Round trip   ahin un tzurik

First class   ershteh klas

Second class   tsvaiteh klas

When do we get to . . .?   Ven kumen mir on kain . . .?

Where is the train to . . .?   Vu iz der tsug kain . . .?
When does it leave?   Ven fort er op?

Where is the dining-car?   Vu iz der vagon-restoran?

Open the window.   Effent dos fenster.
Close the window.   Farmach dos fenster.

Where is the bus to . . .?   Vu iz der otohbus tsu . . .?

I want to go to . . .   Ich vil forn tsu . . .

Please tell me where to get off.   Zeit azoy gut, zogt mir
   vu oystsushtaigen (. . . vu aroptsugaien).

Where is the gas station?   Vu iz der gazolin stantsyeh?

I need gas.   Ich darf hoben gazolin.

I need oil.   Ich darf hoben ail.

Water   vasser

Tires   gumi reder

Something is wrong with the car.   Epes iz kalyeh ge-
   voren mit dem oyto.
Can you fix it?   Kent ir es farrichten?

How long will it take? Vi lang vet es nemen?

Is this the road to . . .? Iz dos der veg kain . . .?

Have you a map? Hot ir a mapeh?

Where is the boat to . . .? Vu iz di shif kain . . .?

When does it leave? Ven gait zi op?

WHEN YOU WANT TO MAKE FRIENDS

Good day. Gut morgen.

My name is. Ich hais.

What is your name? Vi ruft men eich? Vos iz eier nomen? Vi haist ir?

I am delighted to meet you. Ich bin tsufriden eich tsu kenen.

It was a pleasure seeing you. Es iz geven a fargenigen tsu eich zen.

Do you speak English? Ret ir english?

I speak only a little. Ich red nor a bissel.

Do you understand? Tsi farshtait ir?

Please speak slowly. Zeit azoy gut, ret pavolyeh (pamelech).

I am from New York. Ich kum fun niew york.

Where are you from? Fu vanen kumt ir?

I like your country very much. Ich hob eier land zaier lib.

Your city eier shtot

Your house eier haim

Have you been in America? Tsi zeit ir geven in amerike?

This is my first visit here. Dos iz mein ershter bazuch do.

May I sit here? Meg ich doh avegzetsen?

May I take your picture? Meg ich nemen fun eich a bild?

This is a picture of my wife.   Dos iz a bild fun mein veib.

    husband.   man.
    son.   zun.
    daughter.   tochter.
    mother.   mameh.
    father.   tateh.
    sister.   shvester.
    brother.   bruder.
    brother-in-law.   shvoger.
    sister-in-law.   shvegerin.
    father-in-law.   shver.
    mother-in-law.   shviger.
    in-laws.   mechutonim.
    aunt.   mumeh.
    uncle.   feter.
    family.   mishpocheh.

Have you any children?   Hot ir kinder?

How beautiful!   Azoy shain!

Very interesting.   Zaier interesant.

Would you like a cigarette?   Tsi vilt ir a papiros?
    something to drink?   epes tsu trinken?
    something to eat?   epes tsu essen?

Sit down, please.   Zetst zich avek, zeit azoy gut.

Make yourself at home.   Macht zich bakvem.

Good luck!   Mazel tov!

To your health!   Tsu gezunt!

When can I see you again?   Ven ken ich eich zen noch a mol?

Where shall we meet?   Vu zollen mir zich treffen?

Here is my address.   Doh iz mein adres.

What is your address?   Vos iz eier adres.

What is your phone number?   Vos iz eier telefon-numer?

May I speak to . . .?   Ken ich reden mit . . .?

Would you like to have lunch?   Tsi volt is veln essen mitog?
    dinner?   vetshereh?
    a drink?   nemen a trunk?

Would you like to take a walk? Tsi vilt ir gaien
shpatsiren?
    to go to the movies?   tsu gaien in kinoh?
    to the theatre?   in teater?
    to the beach?   tsu der plazhe?

With great pleasure!   Mit grois fargenigen!

I am sorry.   Es fardrist mich.

I cannot.   Ich ken nit.

Another time   an ander mol

I must go now.   Ich muz itst gaien.

Thank you for a pleasant day.   A dank far an
angenemen tog.

Have you a match?   Tsi hot is a shvebeleh?

Thank you for an excellent dinner.   A dank eich far an
oysgetsaichenten moltseit.

This is for you.   Dos iz far eich.

A little souvenir   a klainer ondenk

You are very kind.   Ir zeit zaier gut-hartsik.

It's nothing really.   Es iz be'emes gor nit.

With best regards   mit di beste grussen

Regards home.   A grus in der haim.

Congratulations!   Mazel tov!

WHEN YOU ARE IN TROUBLE

Help!   Gevald!

Police!   Politsai!

Fire!   Es brent!

Stop that man!   Shtelt op dem man!

I have been robbed!   Meh hot mich baroibt!

Look out!   Hit zich!

Wait a minute!   Vart a minut!

Stop!   Hert oyf! Shtelt zich op!

Get out!   Gait aroys!

Hurry up! Eilt zich! Shnell! Macht es gich!

Don't bother me! Tchepeh zich nit tzu mir!

What is going on? Vos tut zich doh?

I don't understand. Ich farshtai nit.

Please speak more slowly. Zeit azoy gut,
 ret pamelecher.

Entrance areingang

Exit aroysgang

Danger! Sakoneh!

Keep out! Meh tor nit araingaien.

No smoking. Nit raicheren.

No parking. Nit parken.

Dead end blindh gessel

One way ain richtung

I am ill. Ich bin krank.

It hurts here. Es tut mir vai doh.

Please call a doctor. Zeit azoy gut, ruft a doktor.

Take me to the hospital. Nemt mich in shpitol.

Where is a drugstore? Vu is doh an apteik?

Where is a dentist? Vu iz a tson-doktor?

I have lost my bag. Ich hob farloyren mein valiz.
 my wallet. mein beitel.
 my passport. mein pass.
 my camera. mein aparat.

I am an American. Ich bin an amerikaner.

Everything is all right. Alts iz gut.

TWO_____

Words
and Phrases
Alphabetized

A a, an
Address adres
Again noch, noch a mol, vider, veiter
Airmail luftpost
Airport fliplats, luftport
All alts, gants, aleh, alemen, ingantsen
All right gut, gants gut
Already shoyn
American amerikaner
And un
And this un dos
Another an andereh
Another time an andereh tzeit, an andersh mol
Any kain
Any mail for me? Iz doh far mir a briv?
Any packages? Zeinen doh peklech?
Anyone emetser
Apothecary apteik
Around arum
Articles (goods) artiklen, zachen

Aunt mumeh

Automobile oyto, otoh,

Bag (pocketbook, wallet) beitel

(Go) back! (Gai) tzurik!

Bad kalyeh, shlecht

Bags bagazh, valizes

Barber shop razeer shtoob

Bath bod, vanneh

Be well! Zei gezunt!

Beach plazheh

Beans fasolyes, beblech, bubkes

Beautiful shain

Beauty parlor shainkeit-salon

Beef stew rinderner-gulash

Beer bir

A better quality a bessereh aigenshaft, a bessereh kvalitet

Bigger gresser

Bill chesben

My bill, please. Mein cheshben, zeit azoy gut.

Black shvarts

Black coffee shvartzeh kaveh

Blue bloy

Boat shif

Bon voyage! Fort gezunterhait!

Book buch

Book store bicher-krom

Bother, v. tchepen

Bread broyt

Bread and butter broyt mit putter

Breakfast frishtik

Bring, v. brengen

Bring me another fork. Brengt mir an anderen gopel.

Bring me some water. Brengt mir a bissel vasser.

Brother bruder

Brother-in-law shvoger

Brown broyn

Building binyen

Bus oytobus, otohbus

Butter putter

Buy koyfen

Cake lekech

To call rufen

Call a doctor. Ruft a doktor.

Call me at seven in the morning. Ruft mich ziben a zaiger in der fri

Camera fotografir-aparat

Can you fix it? Kent ir es farrichten?

Car oyto, otoh

Carrots meren

Cauliflower kalafyoren

Ceiling sufit, pulip, stelyeh

Change (money), v. oysbeiten

Cheap bilig

Cheaper biliger

The check please. Dem cheshben, zeit azoy gut.

Cheese kez

Cheese cake kez-kuchen

Chicken hun

Children kinder

Cigarette papiros

City shtot

Class klas

Clean, adj. rain

Clean, v. rainiken, oysrainiken

Clock zaiger

Close the window. Farmach dos fenster.

Clothing klaider

Coat, topcoat mantel

Cocktail coktail

Coffee kaveh

Coffee with cream kaveh mit shmant

Color kolir

Come kumen

Come back kumen tzurik

Come here. Kumt aher.

Come in. Kumt arein.

Comfortable bakvem

Congratulations! Mazel tov!

Cost kost

Costume kostyum

Costume jewelry kostyum tsirung, kinstleche tsirung

Country land, medinah

Cow ku

Cream krem, smeteneh, shmant

Cucumber ugerkeh

Cutlets kotleten

Darker tunkeler

Daughter tochter

Daughter-in-law shnur

Day tog (sing.), teg (pl.)

Dead end blindeh gessel

Be delighted zein tsufriden

Deliver tsushtelen

Department (of a store) optail

Dentist tsondokter

Department store universal gesheft

Dining car vagon-restoran, vagon ess-tzimmer

Dinner vetshereh

Disappointment entoishung, genart

Do you have hot ir

Do you speak English? Tsi ret ir english?

Do you understand? Tsi farshtait ir?

Doctor dokter

Dollar dolar

Don't bother me! Tshepeh zich op fun mir!

Down the hatch! l'cheiyim

Drink, n. trunk, troonk

Drink, v. trinken

Drug store apteik

Eat, v. essen

Eggs aier

Eight acht

Eighteen achtsen

Eighth achte(r)

Eighty achtsik

Eleven elef

Eleventh elfte(r)

Enough genug

Entrance areingang

Evening ovnt

Everything is all right. Alts iz gut.

Excellent oysgetsaichent

Excuse me. Zeit moichel, antshuldikt mir.

Exit aroysgang

Expect, await dervarten

Family mishpocheh

Fast gich

Father tateh, foter

Father-in-law shver

Fifteen fuftsen

Fifth finfte(r)

Fifty fuftsik

Fire! Es brent!

First ershte(r)

First class ershteh klas

Fish fish

Five finf

Fix farrichten

Floor dil, goren, podlogeh

Floor goren (story level), dil, podlogeh, brik

Flower shop blumen-krom

Food store shpaiz-krom

For far, oyf

For tomorrow oyf morgen

Fork gopel

Forty fertsik

Four fir

Fourteen fertsen

Fourth ferte(r)

Friday freitik

Fried gepregelteh

From fun

From where fun vanen

Fruit frucht

Gasoline gazolin

Gasoline station gazolin-stantsyeh

Glad to meet you. Tsufriden eich tsu kenen.

Gentlemen menner

Get off aropgaien

Get off aropgaien, aroptsugaien, oystsushtaigen

Glass gloz

Glass of beer a gloz bir

Gloves hentchkes

Go gaien

Go away! Gai avek!

Go slow! Pavolyeh! Pamelech!

Good gut

Good-by. A guten. Shalom.

Good day. Gut morgen.

Good evening. Guten ovent.

Good luck! Mazel tov!

Good morning. Gut morgen.

Good night. A guteh nacht.

Gray groy

Great grois

Great pleasure grois fargeniven

Green grin

Hat hut, hitel

Have it delivered. Shikt es tsu. Brengt es tsu.

Have you a map? Hot ir a karte (mapeh)?

Have you been in America? Tsi zeit ir geven in amerike?

Have you children? Tsi hot ir kinder?

He er

Healthy gezunt

Hello! Haloh! Shalom!

Help! Gevald!

Here doh, aher, ot

Here are my bags. Ot iz mein bagazh.

Here is my address. Do is mein adres.

Here is my passport. Ot iz mein pass.

Home   haim

Honey   honik

Honey cake   honik-lekech

Hospital   shpitol

Hot water   haiseh vasser

Hotel   hotel

Hour   sho

How   viazoy

How are you?   Vos macht ir?

How beautiful!   Azoy shain!

How long will it take?   Vi lang vet es nemen?

How much?   Vifil?

How much by the day?   Vifil kost a tog?
Vifil loitn tog?

How much by the hour?   Vifil kost a sho?
Vifil loitn sho?

How much is it?   Vifil kost es?

How much is it to . . .?   Vifil kost es tsu . . .?

Hundred   hundert

Hungry   hungerik

Hurry, v.   eilen zich

Hurry up!   Eilt zich unter! Macht es shnell!
Macht es gich!

Hurt (pain)   vai

Husband   man

I   ich

I am an American.   Ich bin an amerikaner.

I am delighted to meet you.   Es frait mich eich tsu
kenen.

I am disappointed.   Ich bin entoisht. Ich fil zich genart

I am expecting someone.   Ich dervart emetsen.

I am from New York.   Ich kum fun niew york.

I am hungry.   Ich bin hungerik.

I am ill. Ich bin krank.

I am just looking around. Ich kuk zich nor arum.

I am sorry. Es fardrist mich. Es tut mir laid.
Zeit moichl.

I cannot. Ich ken nit.

I come from ich kum fun

I do not understand. Please repeat. Ich farshtai nit.
Zeit azoy gut, chazert es iber.

I don't know. Ich vais nit.

I don't like it. Es gefeit mir nit.

I don't like the color. Der kolir gefelt mir nit.

I don't understand. Ich farshtai nit.

I don't want any sauce. Ich vil nit kain gedempts.

I don't want it. Ich vil es nit.

I have been robbed! Meh hot mich baroibt!

I have lost my wallet (bag). Ich hob farloyren mein
beitel (valiz).

I have two bags. Ich hob tsvai valizes.

I'know. Ich vais.

Like, v. lib hoben; gefelen

I like it. Es gefelt mir.

I like your country very much. Eier land gefelt mir
zaier shtark.

I must go now. Ich muz itst gaien.

I need gas. Ich darf hoben gazolin.

I need it for tonight. Ich darf es oyf heint ovent.

I need oil. Ich darf hoben ail.

I speak only a little. Ich red nor a bissel.

I want ich vil

I want a room. Ich vil a tsimmer.
    with bath. mit a vanneh.
    for one person. far ain mentsh.
    for two persons. far tsvai mentshen.
    for two days. oif tsvai teg.

for a week. oif a voch.

till Monday. biz montik.

I want five airmail stamps for the United States. Ich vil finf luftpost-markes far di farainikteh shtaten.

I want that. Ich vil dos.

I want to change some money. Ich vil oysbeiten a bissel gelt.

I want to eat. Ich vil essen.

I want to go to . . . Ich vil gain tsu . . .

I want to have this washed. Ich vil lozen dos oysvashen.

    pressed. oyspressen.

    cleaned. oysrainiken.

I want to see . . . Ich vil zaien . . .

I want to send a telegram. Ich vil shiken a telegrameh.

I would like ich volt veln

I would like to buy this. Ich volt gevolt dos koyfen.

Ice eiz

Ice cream eiz krem

If az, oyb, tomer, tsi

If anyone calls me, I'll be back at six. Oyb emetser telefonirt mir—ich vel kumen tsurik zeks a zaiger.

I'll take it with me. Ich vel es nemen mit zich.

I'm sorry. Es tut mir laid.

I'm thirsty. Ich bin dorshtik.

In in, arein, oyf

In America my size is in amerike iz mein moz

In the morning in der fri

In-laws (parental) mechutonim

Interesting interesant

Is iz

Is it ready? Es iz fartig?

Is the tip included? Iz dos trinkgelt areingerechent?

Is this the road to . . .? Iz dos der veg kain . . .?

Is this the train for . . .? Iz dos der tsug kain . . .?

It es

It hurts me. Es tut mir vai.

It is very good. Es iz zaier gut.

It was a pleasure seeing you. Es is geven a fargenigen eich tsu zen.

It was very good. Es iz geven zaier gut.

It's all right. Es iz gants gut.

It's nothing really. Es iz be'emes gornit.

It's too much. Es iz tsu fil.

Jewelry tsirung

Juice zaft

Keep out! Meh tor nit araingaien!

Key shlisel

Key, please. Mein shlisel, zeit azoy gut.

Knife messer

Know (facts) vissen

Know (people, languages, skills) kenen

Ladies froyen

Ladies room washtsimmer far froyen

Lamb meat shepsen-flaish

Later shpetter

Leave, depart, v. avek gaien

Left links

Leg fus

Leg of lamb fus fun shepsen-flaish

Lemon limeneh

Letter, mail briv

Lettuce salat

Lighter (color) heler, lichtiker

Like, v. lib hoben, gefelen

Little quantity a bissel

Little size   klain

A little more, please.   A bissel mer, zeit azoy gut.

A little souvenir.   A klainer ondenk.

Long   lang

Look around   kuk arum

Look out, beware, watch out   hiten zich

Look out!   Hit zich!

Lose, v.   farliren

Love, v.   lib hoben

Luck   mazel, glik

Lunch   varrems, mitog

Mail, letter   post, briv

Make yourself at home.   Macht zich bakvem.

Make yourself comfortable.   Macht zich bakvem.

Man   man, mentsh

Map   karteh, mapeh

Match, light   shvebeleh

May I sit here?   Meg ich doh zich avekzetsen?
     speak to . . .?   reden tsu . . .?
     take your picture?   nemen fun eich a bild?

Me   mir

Meat   flaish

Meet   bagegenen

Men   menner, mentshen

Men's clothing   menner-klaider

Men's room   vashtsimmer far menner

Menu   shpaizkart, menyu

Milk   milch

Million   milyon

Mine   mein(er)

Mineral water   mineral vasser

Minute   minut, minoot

Monday montik

Money gelt

More mer

Morning morgen (also means tomorrow)

Morning (early) fri

Mother mameh

Mother-in-law shviger

Movies kinoh

My mein(er)

My name is ich hais

My size is mein moz iz

Name nomen

Need, v. darfen

Night nacht

Nine nein

Nineteen neintsen

Ninety neintsik

Ninth neinte(r)

No nain

No parking. Nit parken. Nit avekshtellen.

No smoking. Nit raicheren.

Not nit, nisht

Not any nit kain

Not so fast! Nit azoy gich!

Nothing gornit

Now itzt, shoyn

Number numer

O'clock a zaiger

Off, down arop

Oil ail

Omelet omlett, fein-kochen

One ains

One hundred hundert

One way ain richtung

   and back un tzurik

Oneself zich

Onions tsibeles

Only nor

Open, v. effenen

Open the window. Effen dos fenster.

Or oder

Orange marants, pomerants, oranzh

Orange juice marantsn-zaft

Out! Aroys!

Out (prefix) oys-

Package pekel

Pair por

Pair of gloves a por hentchkes

Park, v. parken, avekshtellen

Parlor salon

Passport pass

Pastry gebeks

Peas arbes

Pepper feffer

Perfume parfum

Person mentsh (sing.), mentshen (pl.)

Picture bild

Pie flodn

Pink rozeh

Plate teller

Pleasant time eingenemeneh tseit

Please. Zeit azoi gut. Bitteh.

Please, v. gefelen

To be pleased zein tsufriden

Pleasure fargenigen, fraid

Police! Polits! Politsai!

Porter! Treger!

Postage stamps markes

Postcards postkartlech

Potatoes kartofles, bulbes

Press, v. pressen, oyspressen

Put, place, v. laigen

Put it there. Laig es dorten.

Quality kvalitet

Quickly shnell, gich

Railroad train, bahn

> **To the railroad station.** Tsu der ban stantsyeh.
> Tsum vok-zal.

Rain regen

Raincoats regen-mantlen

Rare (meat) nit debroten

Rate of (exchange) koors, kurs

Ready fartig

Receipt kaboleh

Red royt

Red wine royter vein

Regards grus, grussen

Regards home. A grus in der haim.

Relatives mishpocheh

Repeat iberchazeren, nochzogen

Restaurant restoran

Rice reiz

Ride, v. foren (verb)

Right (direction) rechts

Right, correct richtik, gerecht

Road veg

Roasted chicken gebroteneh hun

Rob baroiben

Robbed baroibt

Rolls and Coffee bulkes un (mit) kaveh

Room tsimmer

Round trip ahin un tsurik

Salads salatn

Sale! Oysfarkoyf!

Salt and Pepper zalts un feffer

Sandwich sendvich

Saturday shabbes

Sauce gedempts

Second tsvaiteh (adj.), tsvaiter (n.)

Second class tsvaiteh klas

See you again. Meh vet zich zen.

Self zich

Send shiken

Send breakfast to room 702. Shikt frishtik tsum tsimmer ziben hundert un tsvai.

Seven ziben

Seventh zibete(r)

Seventy zibetsik

She zi

Shirts hemder

Shoes shich

show, v. veizen

Show me another room. Veist mir an anderer tsimmer.

Sickness krenk

Sister shvester

Sister-in-law shvegerin

Sit zitsen

Sit down. Zetst zich avek.

Six zeks

Sixteen zechtsen

Sixth zekste(r)

Sixty zechtsik

Size moz

Slow, slowly pavolyeh, pamelech

Small klain

Smaller klener

Smoke, v. raicheren

So long. Zeit gezunt. Shalom. Meh vet zich zen.

Soap zaif

Socks shkarpeten

Soda sodeh

Sold oysfarkoyft

Some etlecheh, a bissel

Some postcards eltecheh postkartlech

Someone emetser

Something epes

Something cheaper, please. Epes biliger, zeit azoy gut.

Something is wrong with the car. Epes iz kalyeh in dem oyto.

Something to drink? Epes tsu trinken?

Something to eat? Epes tsu essen?

Son zun

Son-in-law aidim

Have sorrow tun bank

Be sorry hoben fardross

Soup zup, yoych

Souvenir ondenk

Speak reden

Speak more slowly. Ret pamelecher.

Speak slowly. Ret pavoli (pamelech).

Spoon   leffel

Sport articles   shport artiklen

Stamps   markes

State   shtat

Steak   ku-flaish, oksen-flaish

Stew   gulash

Stockings   zoken

Stop!   Hert oyf! Shtelt zich op!

Stop here!   Oyfheren doh! Shtelt zich op doh!

Stop that man!   Farhalt dem man! Shtelt op dem man!

Store   krom

Straight   gleich

Straight ahead   fort gleich

Strawberry   trushkaveh

String, cord   shtrik

Sugar   tsuker

Sunday   zuntik

Swiss cheese   shvaitser kez

Table   tish

Table for two   a tish far tsvai

Take   nemen

Take me to the hospital.   Nemt mir in shpitol arein.
    to the hospital.   tsu a shpitol.

Taxi!   taksi!

Tea with lemon   tai mit limeneh

Telegram   telegrameh

Telephone   telefon

Tell   zogen

Tell him (her) to wait for me.   Zog im (ir)az er (zi) zol
    varten oyf mir.

Tell me, where there is a drug store?   Zogt mir vu iz do
    an apteik?

Tell me where to get off. Zogt mir vu aroptsugaien.

Ten tsen

Tenth tsente(r)

Thank you. A dank.

Thank you for a wonderful day. A dank far an angenemen tog.

    for an excellent dinner. far an oysgetsaychenten moltseit.

That dos

That's enough. Shoyn genug.

Theatre teater

There dorten

Third dritte(r)

Thirsty durshtik

Thirteen dreitsen

Thirty dreisik

This dos

This is a picture of my wife. Dos iz a bild fun mein veib.

This is for you. Dos iz far eich.

This is my lrst visit here. Dos iz mein ershter bazuch doh.

Thousand toyzent

Three drei

Thursday donershtik

Ticket bilet

Time tzeit (hour), mol (interval)

Tip trinkgelt

Tires gumi reder

To tsu, tsum

To your health! Tsu gezunt! L'chaiyim!

Toilet klozet, vash-tsimmer

Tomatoes tomaten, pomidoren

Tomorrow **morgen**

Tonight heint ovent, heint bei nacht

Too, also oych, oychet

Too, excessive tsu

Too much tsu fil

Toothpaste tsonpasteh

Towel hantech

Tower turem

Toys shpiltszeig, shpilchelech, tsatskes

Train tsug, ban

Tuesday dinstik

Turn right. Farkerevet zich oyf rechts.

Twelve tsvelf

Twelfth tsvelfte(r)

Twenty tsvontsik

Twenty-one ain un tsvontsik

Two tsvai

Uncle feter

Understand farshtain

Underwear untervesh

United States farainikteh shtaten

Until biz

Up aroyf

Veal kalb-flaish, kelberneh-flaish

Veal cutlets kelberneh-kotleten

Vegetables grins, grinvarg, grinsteig

Very zaier

Very interesting zaier interesant

Very well, thank you, and you? Zaier gut, a dank, un vos macht ir?

Village shtetel

Visit bazuch

Wait varten

Wait a minute! Vart a minut (minoot)!

Wait for me. Vart oyf mir.

Waiter! Kelner!

Waitress! Kelneren!

Walk, v. shpatziren

Wallet beitel

Wash, v. vashen, oysvashen

Watch, clock zaiger

Water vasser

Way, direction veg

Wednesday mitvoch

Week voch

Well, good, fine gut, fain

Well-done (meat) gut durchgebroten

What? Vos? Vossereh?

What do you call this? Vi haist dos?

What is going on? Vos tut zich?

What is good today? Vos iz gut heint?

What is that building? Vos iz der binyen?
  Can it be visited? Ken men in ihm areingain?

What is there for dessert? Vos hot ir far kompot?

What is the rate to the dollar? Vifil iz der koors fun dollar?

What is the telephone number? Vos iz der telefon-numer?

What is there for dessert? Vos hot ir far desert?

What is your address? Vos iz eier adres?

What is your name? Vos ruft men eich? Vos iz eier nomen? Vi haist ir?

What is your phone number? Vos is eier telefon-numer?

What time is it? Vifil halt der zaiger?

What vegetables? Vossereh grins?

When? Ven?

When can I see you again? Ven ken ich eich zen noch a mol?

When do we get to . . . Ven kumen mir on kain . . .

When does it leave? Ven for men op?

When will it be ready? Ven vet es zein fartig?

Where? Vu?

Where from? Fun vanen?

Where to? Vuhin?

Where are you from? Fun vanen kumt ir?

Where can I buy? Vu ken ich koyfen?

Where do I get off? Vu gai ich arop?

Where is a dentist? Vu iz doh a tson-dokter?

Where is a drugstore? Vu iz do an apteik?

Where is the gas station? Vu iz di gazolin-stantsyeh?

Where is a good hotel? Vu iz a guter hotel?

Where is a good restaurant? Vu iz do a guter restoran?

Where is the boat to . . . ? Vu iz di shif kain . . . ?

Where is the bus to . . . ? Vu iz der oytohbus kain . . . ?

Where is the department for . . . ? Vu iz der optail far . . . ?

Where is the dining car? Vu is der restoran vagon?

Where is the ladies' room? Vu iz dos vashtsimmer far froyen?

Where is the men's room? Vu iz dos vashtsimmer far menner?

Where is the telephone? Vu iz der telefon?

Where is the toilet? Vu iz der klozet?

Where is the train to . . . ? Vu iz der tsug kain . . . ?

Where is there ...? Vu iz do ...?

Where shall we meet? Vu zollen mir zich bagegenen?

Whiskey viski, shnaps, bronfen

Whiskey and soda viski mit sodeh

White veis

White wine veisser vein

Wife veib

Window fenster

Wine vein

With mit

With best regards. Mit di beste grussen.

With great pleasure mit a grois fargenigen

With or without sugar? Mit tsuker oder on tsuker?

With potatoes mit kartofles

Without on

Who ver

Wonderful vunderlich

Women's clothing froyen klaider

Would you like to have lunch? Tsi volt ir veln essen varrems?
    a cigarette? a papiros?
    dinner? vetshereh?
    a drink? a trunk (troonk)?

Would you like to go to the movies? Tsi volt ir veln gaien in kinoh?
    to the theatre? in teater?
    to the beach? tsu der plazhe?
    to take a walk? shpatsiren?

Wrong kalyeh

You understand? Farshtaist?

Yellow gel

Yes yoh

You du (sing.), ir, eich (pl.)

You are very kind. Ir zeit zaier gut-hartsik (lib).

You are welcome. Nit do far vos.

Your eier

Your city eier shtot

Your house eier haim, eier hoiz, eier shtub

Your name? Eier nomen? Vi haist ir?

Yourself zich

THREE_____

Popular
Words, Idioms
and Colloquialisms

Absent-minded Aiver butel, oiver botel

Ache, n. vaitik

All at once inmitten drinnen, plootzim

All shoemakers go barefoot. Alleh shusters gaien borves.

Alphabet Alefbais (the first two letters of the Hebrew alphabet)

Amen ohmain

An unlucky person is a dead person. A mentsh on glik iz a toyter mentsh.

Ancestry Yichus

Angel of death der malech hamoves

Angry person kasnik

Animal, dull-witted human being behaimeh

Anniversary of the death of a person Yortseit

Annoy persistently nudgen

Annoying person nudnik, onshikenish

Another man's disease is not hard to endure. A makeh unter yenem's orem iz nit shver tsu trogen. (Lit., a boil in another's arm is not hard to endure.)

Antique altvarg, antik, tranteh

Anything worthless shmatteh (rag), bubkes (beans)

Are you crazy?   Tsi bistu meshugeh?

Are you in a hurry?   Shtaist ahf ain fus? (Lit., are you on one leg?)

As futile as stomping on the earth!   Es iz nit vert a zets in drerd. (Lit., not worth a knock on the earth!)

As long as I can be with you.   Abi tsu zein mit dir.

Ask a sick man!   A kranken fregt men! (i.e., when a man is ill, you ask him what he wants to eat; a humorous reply to a host's offer of refreshments.)

Ask me something else!   Freg mich becherim! (Used when you don't know the answer or are indifferent.)

Assuredly   Takeh

Atonement   kaporeh

Attractive girl   tsatskeh (Lit., toy)

Authority   maivin

Average man   mittelmessiger

Aw, hell!   A broch!

Awkward person   klotz, kuneh-lemel

Back-handed slap   frask

Bad   shlecht

Bad person, someone capable of evil   vos-in-der-kort (Lit., represents every bad card in the deck)

Bad taste!   mein bobbeh's tam (Lit., my grandmother's taste)

Badger, v.   nudgen

Baked dumplings, filled with potato, meat, liver, or barley   knishes

Bang, n.   a chmalyeh, a klap, a zetz

Barely made it!   kom mit tsores! (Lit., barely avoided trouble!)

Bargain, n.   metsiyeh

Bargain, v.   handlen, dingen zich

Bastard   mamser, oisvurf

Be at pains to (please), make an effort   zei zich matriach (make an effort.)

Be happy! Zeit mir frailech!

Be so good zeit azoy gut

Be quiet! Zol zein shtil!

Be well! Zeit mir gezunt. Zeit gezunt!

Beautiful as the seven worlds. Shain vi di ziben velten.
(Legend has it that God made and destroyed the world
seven times before he finally made our world.)

Bedbug vantz

Beet soup borsht

Beggar shnorrer, bettler

Believe me! Gloib mir!

Belly-button pipek, pupik

Bewildered tsetoomelt

Big bargain groisseh metsiyeh

Big boss balebos

Big breadwinner (ironic, of a person who isn't) groisser
fardiner

Big deal! (ironic) Ain klainikeit! (Lit., one small matter)
Gantseh megilah! Groisseh gedillah! A glick hot dich
getrofen!

Big eater fresser

Big good-for-nothing groisser gornisht

Big healthy dame a gezunteh moid

Big mouth! Pisk!

Big noise tararam

Big shot knacker, gantser knacker, groisser shisser

Bit shtik, shtikel

Bitter person farbissener

Blabbermouth (female) yenteh

A black year! (A) shvartz yor!

Blessed with children. Gebentsht mit kinder.

A blessing on your head. A leben ahf dein kop.
(Idiomatically, well said! well done!) A brocheh ahf
dein kop.

Blinding the eyes!   Es shvindilt in di oygen!

Bluff one's way out   unterfonfen

Blundered   farblonjet

Boarding house with cooking privileges   koch-alain

Bologna   vursht

Bon voyage!   Fort gezunterhait!

Book of services for the first two nights of Passover   hagadah, hagodeh (Lit., story)

Boor   yold

Boorish young man   grobber yung

Boorish or coarse person   burvan

Bore   nudnik

Born loser   umglik

Brazenness   chutzpeh

Break a leg!   Brech a fus! Tsebrech a fus!

Bribe (slang)   shmeer

Bride   kalleh

Bride and groom   chossen-kalleh

Bridegroom   chossen

A Brunhilde   a gezinteh moid

Buckwheat   kashe

Buffoon   shmegegi

Bum   trombenik

Bungler   klotz

Burglar   goniff

Burst with frustration   platsn

Business   gesheft

Busy-body   kochleffel

To butter up   untershmeichlen

Buttocks   hinten, inten (slang), toches (taboo)

Call me a "nut."   Ruf mich knak-nissel [nut-cracker]. (Fig., I don't care.)

Capable housewife and homemaker balebosteh, beryeh

Careless dresser shlump

Cash mezumen

Cash only! Don't ask for credit! Ribi-fish, gelt ahfen tish!

Certainly takeh

Circumcision bris

Charity tsedokeh

Chattering yatatata

Cheap billig

Cheap as soup, a real bargain billig vi borsht

Chopped liver gehakteh leber

Chopped meat hak-flaish

Chump yold

Clumsy person klotz, kuneh-lemel

Clutched at the heartstrings klemt beim hartz

Coarse person grobber yung

Coat, as with butter shmeeren

Coffee cake, pastry gebeks

Come now! Gait, gait!

Come to the point! Macht es keilechdik un shpitsik. (Lit., make it round and pointy.)

Come-upper oyfgekumener, alrightnik (American)

Commandment mitsveh

Common sense, good sense saichel

Compassion rachmones

Complain kvetshen

Complain (when there is nothing to complain about) A chissoren di kaleh iz tsu shain. (Lit., the bride is too pretty.)

Complainer kvetsher, kloger

Complete details gantseh megillah (slang)

Compulsive eater fresser

Conceited ongeblozzen

Confusing work ongepatshket (Lit., muddled)

Confusion kashe (slang) (Lit., mush cereal, buckwheat, or porridge), mishmash, tumel

Congratulations! Mazel tov!

Connoisseur maivin

Continuous eater of snacks nasher

Corny shmaltzik

Costly teier

Could be ken zein

Countryman, fellow townsman landsman

Crazy meshugeh, tsidrait

Crazy antics or actions, a craze or madness meshugass

Crazy as a loon meshugeh ahf toyt

Crazy man meshugener

Crazy woman meshugeneh

Crazy world a meshugeneh velt

Cream smetteneh, shmant (for coffee)

Creep, n. zhlob

Criminal, thief, racketeer gazlen

Cripple kalyekeh

Crook goniff, ganev

Crooked actions Ganaivisheh shtiklech

A curse on my enemies A klog tsu meineh sonim.

A curse on you. A broch ahf dir. A choleryeh ahf dir. A finster yor ahf dir.

Customary gifts exchanged on Purim, usually candy, cake shalach mohnes

Cut it short! On langeh hakdomes! (Lit., without long introductions)

Cute (girl) lyalkeh, tsatskeh (Lit., plaything, doll)

Daddy tateh

Dairy food milchiks (n.), milechdik (adj)

Damn it! A broch!

Darling neshomeleh, teiers

Dear teier

Delicacy meichel

Delicious tasting geshmak

The devil with him! Ich hob im in bod!

Dietary laws kashress

Diminutive, affectionate term for children kinderlach

Diplomacy saichel, diplomatyeh

Dipped eingetunken

Dirt shmuts

Disappointment entoishung, fardross

Do it fast! Mach es shnell!

Do it for my sake. Tu mir tsulib.

Do me a favor. Tu mir tsulib. Tu mir a toiveh.

Do me a favor and drop dead! Folg mich a gang un gai in drerd!

Do you want? Vilstu?

Doll lyalkeh, tsatskeh, krassavitseh (beautiful girl)

Dolt shnook

Don't be a damn fool! Zei nit kein vyzosoh!

Don't be a fool! Zeit nit kain nar! Zeit nit kain goilem!

Don't bleed me! Tsap mir nit dos blut! (Fig., don't aggravate me.)

Don't bother me! Drai mir nit kain kop! Hak mir nit kain tsheinik! Tshepeh zich nit tsu mir! Tshepeh zich op fun mir!

Don't complain. Zindik nit. Baklog zich nit.

Don't do me any favors. Tu mir nit kain toyves.

Don't double-talk. Nisht gefonfet.

Don't envy. Zindik nit. Zai nit mekaneh.

Don't fool around. Nisht gefonfet.

Don't give me an evil eye.   Gib mir nit kain einoreh (eiyin horeh).

Don't make a big deal out of it!   Mach nit kain tsimmes [sweet carrot compote] fun dem!

Don't mix up the prayers.   Farmisht nit di yotsres.

Don't threaten me!   Strasheh mich nit!

Don't twist my head!   Drai mir nit kain kop!

Don't worry!   Deigeh nisht! Hob nit kain deiges! Nisht gedeiget! Zorg zich nit!

Door post container of parchment on which is written Deuteronomy VI, 4-9 and XI, 13-21   Mezuzeh

Dope   shmendrik, yold

Dopey, clumsy person   shlemiel

Double-talk, v.   fonfen

Dowdy, gossipy woman   barederkeh, recheelisnitseh

Dowry   nadan

Drop dead!   Geharget zolstu verren! Ver derharget! Ver geharget! Ich hob dich! Zolst ligen in drerd!

Drunkard   shicker

Dullard   temper kop

Dull person, clumsy and sluggish   Goilem

Dull-witted   behaimeh (Lit., domesticated animal)

Dumb like a piece of wood!   Shtik holtz!

Dumbbell, dunce, dumb head   dumkop, shtik holtz

Eat voraciously, like an animal   fressen

Eat in good health!   Ess gezunterhait!

Embittered person   farbissener

Enough is enough!   Genug is genug!

The end of the world.   Ek velt.

Endearing term   bubeleh, bubee

Engaged couple   chossen-kalleh

Esteem   koved

Erudite person   lamden

Exciting person kasnik

Excuse me. Zeit (mir) moychel.

Exhausted oysgehorevet, oysgematert

Expensive teier

Expert maivin

Extreme pleasure fargenigen

Fairy tale bobbeh meisseh (Lit., grandmother's story)

Fait accompli a nechtiger tog (Lit., a yesterday's day), farfallen

Fall guy shlump

False or forced laugh. Me lacht mit yashtsherkes.

Family mishpocheh

The faster the better. Vos gicher alts besser.

Fat shmaltz

Father-in-law shver

Feces, dung drek (taboo)

Female infant (affectionate term) pisherkeh (Lit., little urinator)

Female tricks veiberishe shtik

Festive yontefdik

Fidget Sitzen ahf shpilkes. (Lit., to sit on pins and needles)

Filthy rich shtain reich (Lit., gem rich)

Finicky aidel gepatshket (adj.), pritsteh (fem. n.)

Fiftieth wedding anniversary goldeneh chasseneh

Fine balebatish

Flattery shmaltz (slang), komplimenten

Flavor ta'am

Food forbidden under Jewish dietary laws traif

Food that meets rules of Jewish dietary laws kosher

Fool, n. nar, shlemiel, shmendrik, shmegegi, behaimeh

A fool feels nothing. A nar filt nit.

Foolish (fruitless) question klotz kasheh

Foolishness narishkeit

For better, for worse tsum glik, tsum shlimazel

For nothing umzist

Forget him! Ich hob im in bod! (Lit., I have him in the bath)

Fractured English tsebrochener english

Friendly face haimisher ponim

From your mouth to God's ear! Fun eier moyl in Gots oyeren.

Fuss over nothing, n. tsimmes

Gadabout kochleffel

Gall chutspeh

Garden of Eden, paradise ganaiden

Get a move on! Gib zich a shockel! Gib zich a traisel! Eilt zich!

Get away from me! Tshepeh zich op fun mir!

Get killed! Ver derharget! Ver geharget!

Get lost! Go away! Ver farblondjet! Trog zich op!

Getting senile aiver butel, oiver botel

Gimmick machareikeh

Girl of marriageable age kalleh-moid

Gizzard pipek, pupik

Glass of tea glezel tai

Gnawing, grinding person grizhidiker

Go away! Gai avek!

Go bang your head against the wall! Gai klop zich kop in vant!

Go break a leg! Tsebrech a fus!

Go drive yourself crazy! Fardrai zich dein aigenem kop!

Go flap your ears! Ich hob dich! (Lit., I have you [somewheres!])

Go jump in a lake! Nem zich a vanneh! (Lit., take a bath.)

Go mix yourself up, not me! Gai fardrai zich dein aigenem kop!

Go peddle your fish elsewhere! Gai feifen ahfen yam! (Lit., go whistle on the ocean)

Go take a bath! Nem zich a vanneh!

Go to hell! Gai in drerd arein! Ich hob dich in drerd! Gai kabenyeh matyereh!

Go to the devil! A ruach in dein taten's tateh!

Goad utz

Go-between mekler

God forbid! Cholileh! Got zol uphiten! Nisht gedacht! Chas vesholem!

God in Heaven, Master of the Universe! Roboynoy shel oylom!

God knows Got vaist

God should hear you and favor you! Fun eier moyl in Got's oyeren!

God watches out for fools. Got hit op di naronim.

God will punish. Got vet shtrofen.

God willing! Im yirtseh hashem! Mirtsishem!

Going into labor to give birth gaien tzu kind

The golden count y. Goldeneh medina.

Good deed mitsveh

Good for nothing! Toigen ahf kapores!

Good health to you! A gezuntt ahf dein kop!

Good holiday! Gut yontev!

Good Jew shainer yid, a getrayer yid

Good luck! Zol zein mit glik.

Good luck to you! A glik ahf dir!

The good old days mellech sobyetskis yoren (Lit., the years of King Sobieski)

Good Sabbath Gut shabbes.

Good taste taam

Gossip reden rechiless

Gourmet's delight   meichel

Grandfather   zaideh

Gratification, as from children   naches

Grease   shmaltz

Great pleasure, great satisfaction   mecheiyeh

Groans   krechts

A guilty person is always sensitive.   Ahfen goniff brent dos hittel. (Lit., on a thief burns his hat.)

A guy who doesn't smell too good   a shtinker

Hanger-on   nuchshlepper, tsutsheppenish

Happy Sabbath.   Gut shabbes.

Happy-go-lucky, lively world.   A lebedikeh velt.

Having a ball!   Lebt a tog! (Lit., lives a day)

Hard-luck guy who is a sucker for anything, an incompetent, a misfortunate   shlimazel

Hard-working, efficient, housewife   beryeh, balebosteh

Have respect!   Hob derech erets!

He bluffs his way out.   Er fonfet unter.

He eats like a horse.   Er esst vi a ferd.

He eats like a man who has recovered from a sickness.   Er esst vi noch a krenk.

He has a cold!   Er hot a farshtopteh nonjeh. (Lit., he has a stuffed nose.) Er iz farkeelt.

He has strange ways.   Er hot modneh drochim.

He has nothing at all.   Er hot a makeh [boil]. Er hot kadoches.

He hasn't got a worry.   Er hot nit kain zorg.

He is barely able to creep.   Kam vos er kricht.

He makes a lot of trouble for me.   Er macht mir a shvartzeh chasseneh. (Lit., he makes me a black wedding.)

He repeats himself, he re-hashes things over and over again.   Er molt gemolen mel.

He ruins it.   Er macht a tel derfun.

He should drop dead! Paigeren zol er!

He should go to hell! Er zol gaien in drerd! Er zol einemen a misseh meshuneh! (Lit., he should meet a strange death!)

He should have lots of trouble! Er zol zain ahf tsores! Er zol ainemen a miesseh meshuneh!

Having no end of trouble hoben tsu zingen un tsu zogen (Lit., having [enough] to sing and to recite)

He talks himself into a sickness. Er ret zich ein a krenk.

He talks nonsense. Er ret in der velt arein.

He turns the world upside down. Er kert iber di velt.

Hebrew school talmud torah

The hell with it! Ich hob es in drerd!

He's a low-down good-for-nothing. Er iz a nidertrechtiker yung. Er iz an oysvurf.

He's thick. Er hot a farshtopten kop. (Lit., he has a stuffed head.)

He's worthless. Er toyg ahf kapores.

Headache Kop-vaitik

Healthy as a horse gezunt vi a ferd

Heartache hartsvaitik

Hearty laugh hartsik gelechter

Help! Oy gevald! (cry of anguish, distress, suffering, or frustration)

Hole in the head loch in kop

Holiday yontiff, yom tov, yontev (n.), yontefdik (adj.)

Honor, n. koved

Honorable balebatish, choshev

Horrible ending finsterer sof (Lit., dark end)

Horrible year finster yor

Hot bath haiseh vanneh

Hot-head kasnik

Competent housewife beryeh, balebosteh

How are things? How goes it?   Vi gaits? Vos hert zich?

How should I know?   Freg mich becherim!

How's business?   Vi gait dos gesheft?

Hurry up!   Eilt zich! Mach es shnell!

I am disappointed.   Ich bin entoisht. Ich feel zich opgenart.

I am fainting.   Es vert mir finster in di oygen. (Lit., it's getting dark before my eyes.)

I despise you.   Ich hob dich in bod. (Lit., I have you in the bath.)

I don't envy you.   Ich bin dir nit mekaneh.

I don't give a care. I don't give a hang.   A deigeh hob ich.

I don't know.   Ich vais nit.

I do not begrudge you.   Ich bin dich nit mekaneh.

I hate him.   Ich hob im feint.

I have a choice?   A braireh hob ich?

I have a heartburn.   Es brent mir ahfen harts.

I have no use for it.   Ich darf es ahf kapores.

I haven't the faintest idea!   Zol ich azoy vissen fun tsores! (Lit., May I know about troubles [as I know about what you're asking].)

I like it.   Es gefelt mir.

I need it like a hole in my head!   Ich darf es vi a loch in kop.

I need it like a wart on my nose.   Ich darf es vi a lung un leber ahfen noz. (Lit., I need it like a lung and liver on my nose.)

I predicted it. My heart told me.   Dos harts hot mir gezogt.

I should know from trouble as much as I know about that.   Zol ich azoy vissen fun tsores.

I should have such good luck.   Az a glik ahf mir.

I should worry.   A deigeh hob ich.

Idler   laidik-gaier

Idiot   shmegegi (slang)

I'm dying for it.   Mein cheiyes gait oys.

I'm making a fool of myself.   Ich mach zich narish.

I'm not in a hurry.   Ich yog zich nit.

I'm sorry.   Es tut mir bank. Es tut mir laid.

Impossible!   A nechtiker tog! Ummeglich!

Inexpensive   billik, billig

Infant   pisherkeh (f.), pisher (m.) (colloq.)

Inferior merchandise or work   shlak

In-law (parent)   mechuten (sing.), mechutonim (pl.)

In the middle of   in mitten drinnen

Insincere talk   shmaltz (slang)

In spite of everything you do, it still comes out wrong.
Ahf tsu luches. Ahf tsu lehaches.

In trouble   ahf tsores

Is it my worry?   A deigeh hob ich?

Is that how you talk to a father?   Azoy ret men tsu a
taten?

Is that so?   Azoy zogstu? (Lit., that's what you say?)

Is that so? Really?   Takeh?

Israel   eretz yisroel

It appears to me   es veist zich mir oys

It could be.   Es ken zein.

It doesn't matter to me.   Es macht mir nit oys.

It doesn't work!   Es gait nisht! Gait es nit!

It gives me a great pleasure! (also ironic)   Es tut mir a
groisseh hanoeh!

It hurts me.   Es tut mir vai.

It is not fitting.   Es past nit.

It is said.   Meh zogt.

It is very expensive.   Es is zaier teier.
    inexpensive.   billig.

It isn't proper.   Es past nit.

It isn't running smoothly! Es gait nit.

It seems veist oys

It makes no difference. It doesn't matter. Es macht nit oys.

It never happened. Es iz nit geshtoigen un nit gefloigen. (Lit., it didn't stand and it didn't fly.)

It pleases me. Es gefelt mir.

It should be that way. Alevei.

It should happen to me! Ahf mir gezogt gevorn! Alevei ahf mir! Mirchishem bei mir!

It shouldn't come to pass! Nit gedacht gevorn!

It shouldn't happen! Nit gedacht!

It shouldn't happen to us! Nit oyf undz gedacht!

It shouldn't happen to you! Nit oyf eich gedacht!

It sorrows me. Es tut mir bang. (bank)

It stinks. Es gait a raiech. Se hert zich a raiech.

It will all work out. Es vet zich alts oispressen.

It will heal before the wedding. Es vet zich oyshailen far der chasseneh.

It will help like blood-cupping on a dead body. Es vet helfen vi a toiten bankes!

It won't hurt in making a catch. Nit shaten tsum shiddech.

It's a shame for the children. Es iz a shandeh far di kinder.

It's a steal. A metsiyeh fun a goniff. (Lit., a bargain from a thief)

It's bad manners. Es past zich vi a patsh tsu gut shabbes.

It's delicious! Meh ken lecken di finger!

It's good for nothing! Es toig ahf kapores! need it for a [profitless] sacrifice.)

It's great! S'iz mir gut! Es iz mir gut!

It's hardly worth the trouble. Folg mich a gang. (Scoffing statement, lit., follow me on a [useless] errand.)

It's not to the point. Es past zich vi a patch tzu gut shabbes.

It's O.K. with me. Bei mir poilst du.

It's on his (her) mind. Es ligt im (ir) in zinnen.

It's perfect. Kosher veyosher.

It's tough to make a living. Shver tzu machen a leben.

It's useless! Gai klop zich kop in vant! (Lit., go bang your head against the wall.)

It will take a long, long time. Till doomsday. A yor mit a mitvoch. (Lit., a year and a Wednesday)

It's worth nothing. Es toig ahf kapores.

Jewish head yiddisher kop

Jewish native of Galicia galitsianer

Jewish parochial school yeshiva

Jewish prayer shawl tallis

Joy, as from children naches

Joyous occasion: birth, bar mitzvah, engagement, marriage simcheh

Just made it. Kam derlebt.

Keep moving! Drai zich!

Keep quiet! Shveig!

Knock on wood, no evil eye. Kain enoreh. Kain eiyin horeh.

Know-it-all (ironic) maivin

Kosher condition kashress

Leave me alone! Loz mich tsu ru!

Lecherous old man alter kacker (taboo)

Let it be! Zol zein!

Let me be in peace! Loz mich tsu ru!

Let's end it! A sof, a sof!

Let's have some quiet! Zol zein shtil!

Liar ligner

Listen here! Hert zich ein!

Littered ongevorfen

Little bird faigeleh

Little bride kallehnyu

Little cakes dipped in honey taiglech

Little girl (affectionate diminutive) maideleh

A little joy a shtik naches

Little ones pitsilech

Little prig klainer gornisht

Livelihood parnosseh

Lively world lebedikeh velt

Living doll yungeh tsatskeh

Living high off the hog! Leben a chazerishen tog!

Long coat worn by religious Jews kapotah, kaftan

Look at him! Kuk im on!

Loquacious Yatatata

Lost farblondjet

A lot to tell, little to hear. A sach tsu reden, vainik tsu heren.

Loudmouth pisk

Lousy nit gut

Lout grobber yung

Low-life parech (Lit., scab-headed, having sores on the scalp)

Lump of sugar shtik tsuker

Madness meshugass

Make a living machen a leben
   livelihood parnosseh

Make it snappy! Mach es shnell!

Making an outcry machen a gevald

Man built like an ox boorvan

Man who constantly builds castles in the air, man who starves by his wits luftmentsh

Manure drek (taboo)

The marriage is off! Oys shiddech!

Marriage broker shadchen

May God help me! Zol Got mir helfen!

May he break a leg! Zol er tsebrechen a fuss!

May he rest in peace. Olov hasholem. (Lit., in Hebrew, upon him be peace.)

May it not come upon you. Lo alaichem.

May no evil befall us! Kain einoreh!

May she rest in peace. Oleho hasholem.

May you live long. Lang leben zolt ir.

May we meet on happy occasions. Mir zollen zich bagegenen ahf simches.

Mean person paskudnyak

Meat or meat products flaishik (n.), flaishidick (adj.)

Meddlesome spectator kibbitzer

Mercy rachmones

Mess (slang) kashe, mishmash, hekdish

A middleman, one who is neither smart nor dumb mittelmessiger

Miserable finster un glitshik (Lit., dark and slippery)

Misery tsores

Misfortune umglik

Mix-up kashe (slang)

Mixed up tsidrait, farmisht, tsetoomelt

Mixture mishmash

Moans, v. krechts, kvetsht zich

Money gelt, mezumen

Money goes to money. Gelt gait tsu gelt.

Money thrown out, wasted aroysgevorfeneh gelt

Money tied in a corner of a handkerchief knippel

Moron zhlobb

Mortally insane! Meshugah ahf toyt!

Mother-in-law shvigger

Mother's favorite tsatskeleh der mamehs

Mourning period (seven days) shiva

Mouth pisk (slang)

Mr. Slowpoke Kam vos er kricht.

Mr. Upside Down (a person who does everything wrong) moisheh kapoyer

Much ado about nothing! Ahfen himmel a yarid! (Lit., in heaven there's a fair!)

Muddled ongepatshket

My enemies should live so! Meineh sonim zollen azoy leben!

My heart told me! Dos harts hot mir gezogt!

My money went down the drain! In drerd mein gelt! (Lit., into the earth [went] my money!)

Naive person kuneh-lemel

Narrowly achieved kam derlebt

Nasty fellow paskudnyak

Ne'er-do-well. zhlook, trombenik

Neighbor from the old country landsman (sing.) landsleit (pl.)

Neutral food, neither meat nor dairy parveh

Nibble between meals nash

Nibbler, especially between meals nasher

Nincompoop zhlook, shmendrik

No evil eye. Kain einoreh.

No-gooder trombenik

Nobody, a pitiable person nebbach (nebbish), vantz (Lit., bedbug)

Noise tumel

Noise-maker tumler

Non-kosher traif

Non-Jew goy (m), goyeh (f.)

Non-Jew who does work forbidden to observant Jews on the Sabbath Shabbes goy

Non-Jewish boy shaigetz

Non-Jewish girl shikseh

Nonsense! A nechtiker tog! (Lit., a yesterday's day)

Noodle or bread suet pudding kugel

Noodles lokshen

Not good nish gut, nit gut

Not really at all! Chas v'cholileh!

Not so bad nishkosheh

Not today, not tomorrow. Nit heint, nit morgen.

Nothing came of it! Es hot zich oysgelozen a boydem! (Lit., there's nothing there but a small attic.)

Nothing, of small value kreplach (Slang, lit., ravioli), bobkes

Nothing to be sorry for. A shaineh, raineh, kaporeh (Lit., a beautiful, clean sacrifice).

Nothing will help you! Es vet dir gornit helfen!

Nouveau riche oyfgekumener (Lit., come-upper)

Nuisance nudnik, a tsutsheppenish

The nuisance is here already! Er iz shoyn do, der nudnik!

"Nutty" tsidrait

O.K. zaier-gut; zol zein azoy

Obey me. Folg mich.

Oh, God! Gottenyu!

Old acquaintance an alter bakanter

Old witch an alteh machashaifeh

Old wreck an alter trombenik

On the level, true emes

One who is helpless on a job a kalyekeh

One who drops whatever he touches a gelaimter

One who stirs up trouble kochleffel

One who tends to confuse you draikop

Only God knows. Nor Got vaist!

Onions should grow from your navel! Zol vaksen
tsibelis fun pupik!

Other world yeneh velt

Out of this world Ek velt

Overdressed woman iberzaltseneh tsatskeh

Over-praise shmaltz (slang)

Overflow with pride and happiness kvellen

Owner balebos

Pale as a sheet. Blaich vi di vant. (Lit., pale as the
wall.)

Palsy-walsy aderabe-ve'aderabe

Panhandler shnorrer

A patsy shnook, shlump

Parvenu oyfgekumener g'vir

Pauper kaptsen

Pedigree yichus

Peeved, pouting ongeblozen

Perfect kosher (slang)

Person from Lithuania litvak

Person who butts into everything kochleffel

Person with a sweet tooth nasher

Pest tsutsheppenish

Pesty nagger nudnik

Philanthropic spirit tsedokeh

**Phylacteries (worn on head and left arm each weekday
morning while praying)** tefillen

Pig, piggish person chazzer

A pig remains a pig. A chazzer bleibt a chazzer.

Pig's feed, bad food chazzerei

Piece shtik

Piece of luck glick, mazel

A piece of luck happened to you! A glick hot dich
getrofen!

Pious person tsaddik

Pity rachmones

A plague! A finsternish! (Lit., a darkness!)

Plaything tsatskeh

Pleasantly plump and pretty woman zaftig (adj.)

Please. Ich bet eich. Zeit zich matriach. Zeit azoy gut.

Please forgive me. Zeit (mir) moichel.

Please, I beg you. Ich bet eich, bitteh.

Policeman shames (Slang, lit., a synagogue sexton.)

Poor box in the home for odd coins, usually deposited on Friday afternoon, before the Sabbath begins pushkeh

Porridge kashe

Poverty orem-keit

Prayer book sidder

Prayer in honor of the dead kaddish
(begins: Yiskadal veyiskadash)

Pretends to be ignorant. Macht zich nit vissendik.

Prettier ones they bury! The girl is ugly. Sheners laigt men in drerd.

Procrastinating Kum ich nit heint, kum ich morgen!
(Lit., if I don't come today, I'll come tomorrow!)

Proper kosher (slang)

Prostitute nafkeh, kurveh

Proud shtoltz

Puffed up, peeved ongeblozzen

Pull, or carry an unnecessary object shleppen

Punch chmalyeh, klap, zets

Punk, (n.) paskudnyak

Push shtup

Put up or shut up! Toches ahfen tish! (taboo)

Quickly, quickly shnell

Quiet! Shveig! Sha!

Quite a job!   Folg mich a gang!

Rabbi's wife   rebbetsin

Rabid fan, ardent participant   farbrenter

Racketeer   gazlen (Slang, lit., thief), untervelt mensh

Rag   shmatteh

Raise cain   hulyen

The real article, the real McCoy   richtiker chaifets, di emeseh skhoireh

Real bargain   billik vi borsht (Lit., cheap as beet soup)

Really! Is that so!   Tahkeh!

Reciting prayers over lit candles   bentshen lecht

Reciting the afternoon prayers   Davenen mincheh

Relatives   mishpocheh, kroivim

Relatives through marriage, in-law   mechuten (sing.) mechutonim (pl.)

Religious functionary who performs the circumcision   moihel

Remember?   Gedainkst?

Respect   koved, derech erets

Responsible   balebotish

Reverence   koved

Right   kosher (slang)

Righteous person   tsaddik

Ritual bath (part of the bride's wedding preparation)   mikveh

Ritual slaughterer of animals and fowl   shochet

Rogue   yungatsh

Rude young man   grobber yung

Become ruined   verren a tel

Sacrifice   kaporeh

Satisfactory   nishkosheh

To ruin you, to make a nothing out of you   machen a tel fun dir

Scatterbrain draikop

Scholar lamden

School shul

Scram! Gai shoyn, gai!

Scream kvitsh

Screwy tsidrait

Scroll, or Book, of Esther; slang for meaningless rigamarole megillah

Second-rater shlump

Selfmade fool shmok (taboo)

Senile aiver butel, oiver botel

Sentimental shmaltzik, zeeslech

Serves him right! Gut oyf im!

Shame and disgrace a shandeh un a charpeh

Sharp practices genaivisheh shtiklech

She has all the virtues. Alleh meiles hot zi,

Shoddy shlok

To shout for help machen a gevald

Shove, v. shtuppen

Show-off, n. knacker

Shrew shlecht veib

Shriek kvitsh

Shut up! Sha! Shveig!

Shy person nebbach (nebbish)

Sick krank

Sickness krenk

Sickness that hangs on a farshleptch krenk (Lit., a drawn-out sickness)

Silence! Zol zein shtill!

Simpleton nebbach (nebbish), shlemiel

Sit in mourning zitsen shiveh ([Lit., to sit seven,] the number of days in the mourning period)

Sitting on pins and needles zitsen ahf shpilkes

Skin someone alive   reissen flaish

Skull cap worn during prayers, and at all times by Orthodox Jews to indicate that God is present above   yarmelkeh

Slam!   Chmalyeh!

Slap, smack   patsh

Slightly drunk   farshnoshkit

Slime, dirt   shmuts

Slob   zhlob

Slow as molasses.   Kam vos er kricht.

Small pieces of baked dough   taiglech

Small pockets of dough filled with chopped meat or cheese   kreplach

Smell   shmek

Smell badly   farshtunken

A smell and a taste (ironic, in expressing inordinately small amounts)   a lek un a shmek

Smelled bad, as food   shtark gehert (Lit., strongly hear)

Smoked salmon   lox, laks

Snack   nash

So? Well?   Nu?

So I guessed wrong!   Nit getrofen!

So I made a mistake, so what!   Hostu bei mir an avleh!

So it goes.   Azoy gait es.

Something delicious   mecheiyehdik, geshmak

Soul   neshomeh

Sour cream   zoiyereh smetteneh, shmant

Speak nasally, unclearly   fonfen

Special bit of acting   shtik

Spectator who offers unsolicited advice   kibbitzer

Spirit   neshomeh

Spitefully   ahf tsu lehaches

Split your guts! Plats!

Sponger shnorrer, shlepper

"Stacked" (slang) zaftig

Starved toit hungerik

Steam bath a shvitz bod

Stinks, rotten ipish (Aramaic for rotten)

Stomach ache boych-vaitik

Stop annoying me. Drai mir nit kain kop! (Lit., don't turn my head); Hak mir nit kain tsheinik! (Lit., don't knock me any tea-kettle!)

Stop bending my ear! Hak mir nit in kop (Lit., don't knock me in the head!)

Stop talking! Shveig!

A strange death. A miesseh meshuneh. (Fig., it shouldn't happen to a dog.)

Strong kreftig, shtark

Strong character shtarker charakter

Strong as a horse shtark vi a ferd

Stuffed farshtopt, ongeshtopt

Stuffed derma kishkeh

Stuffed fish, usually made of chopped fish, onions and seasoning and cooked in salt water gefilteh fish

Stuffed shirt (slang) ongeblozzener

Sweet cream smetteneh

Swill chazzerei

Sucker shlump, shnook, shlemiel

Suffix denoting diminutive or affection el, elleh

Summer boarding house with cooking privileges koch-alain

Sweet carrot compote tsimmes

Sweetheart neshomeleh (my soul), geleebteh

Sweet soul ziseh neshomeh

To swindle shmeikel

Swindler ganef, shvindler

Swollen, puffed up geshvollen

Synagogue shul

Tact saichel, takt

Take it easy! Chap nit!

Talk, n. shmooz, shmuess

Talk onself into sickness! Zich einreden a krenk!

Talk to the wall (for all the good it will do you)! Red tsu der vant!

Talk your heart out! Red zich oys dos harts!

Tall story bobbeh meisseh

Tasty geshmak

Teamster balagoleh

Teats tsitskes (taboo)

Teen-age girl yung maidel

A terrible thing! Gevaldikeh zach! Shrekliche zach!

Thank God! Danken Got! Got tsu danken! Boruch Hashem!

Thanks for nothing! A shainem dank in pupik! A gezunt in dein pupik! (Lit., thanks in your belly-botton)

That's all. Dos is alts.

That's how it goes. Azoy gait es.

That's nothing. Ez iz bloteh. (Lit., it is mud)

That's worthless. Ez iz bloteh.

There's a buzzing in my head! Es zshumet mir in kop!

They don't let you live! Meh lost nit laiben!

They say! Meh zogt.

Thief goniff, ganef, gazlen

This pleases me. Dos gefelt mir.

This too is a living? This you call a living? Oych mir a leben?

This was a pleasure! Dos is geven a mecheiyeh!

Tickle a kitsel

Tipsy farshnoshkit

Tired out oysgematert

Too bad! Az och un vai!

Too bad the bride is too pretty; a novel complaint A chissoren di kaleh iz tsu shain.

Too late! Noch ne'eleh! Tsu shpait!

Tough guy a shtarker

Tough•luck! Az och un vai!

Tragedy umglik

Treasury of Jewish law interpreting the Torah (five books of Moses) into livable law talmud

Tricky doings genaivisheh shtiklech

Treat meichel, nash

Triflings bobkes

Troubles tsores

Uncouth grob

Uncouth young man grobber yung

Ugly mies

Unfortunate person an umgliklecher mentsh

Ungraceful person klotz

Unkempt, sweaty shlumperik

Unlucky one umglik

An unlucky person is a dead person. A mentsh on glik iz a toyter mentsh.

Unmarried girl maidel (young), moid (older)

Untidy person an opgelozener mentsh

Unwanted follower nuchshlepper

Uproar tumel

Urine pishechtz (taboo)

Utter misery gehakteh tsores

Vicious animal (usually, an inhumane person) baizeh cheiyeh

Vulgar, unmannered man grobyan

Wail of sorrow   Gevald! Och un vai!

Wallop   klap

Wandered around   arumgevalgert

Watch out, to mind   varfen an oyg (Lit., to cast an eye on)

We shall say grace.   Mir vellen bentshen.

Weakling   nebbach (nebbish)

Wear it in good health!   Trog es gezunterhait!

Well done! Well said!   A leben ahf dein kop! (Lit., life to your head!)

Well said.   Zaier shain gezogt.

What a sober man has on his mind (lit., lung), a drunkard has on his tongue.   Vos bei a nichteren oyfen lung, is bei a shikkéren oyfen tsung.

What are you talking my head off for?   Vos hakst du mir a kop? (Lit., what are you knocking [at] my head?)

What are you saying?   Vos zogt ir?

What are they lacking?   Vos failt zai?

What did I need it for?   Vos hob ich dos gedarft?

What difference does it make?   Vos macht dos oys?

What difference does it make as long as he makes a living?   Nifter-pifter a leben macht er? ("Nifter" means a dead man)

What does it matter?   Vos zol es arren?

What does it lead to?   Vos iz der tachlis?

What does it matter to you?   Vos art es eich?

What does it mean?   Vos maint es?

What else?   Vos noch?

What is going on? What's cooking?   Vos tut zich?

What is the name of?   Vi ruft men? Vos haist es?

What will be, will be.   Vos vet zein, vet zein.

What's new.   Vos hert zich epes neiyes?

What's on his mind is on his tongue.   Vos iz in kop iz ahfen tsung!

What's wrong with you? Vos iz mit dir?

What's the outcome? What's the point? Vos iz di untershteh shureh?

What's the purpose? Vos iz der tachlis?

What's the trick? Vos iz di chochmeh?

Where are you going? Vuhin gaistu?

Where does it hurt? Vu tut dir vai?

Where the devil says good morning vu der ruach zogt gut morgen

Whom are you kidding? Vemen barestu?

Whine, n. klog

Whiskey bronfen, shnapps

Who knows! Freg mich becherim! Ver vaist?

Who would have believed it? Ver volt dos geglaibt?

Whole works shmeer, megillah (slang)

Why should I do it? Folg mich a gang. (Scoffiing; lit., follow me on a [useless] errand.)

Wild man! Vilder mentsh!

Wisdom chochmeh

Wise guy knacker

Wise man chochem

Witticism vitz, chochmeh (also used ironically)

Woe is me! Oy, vai iz mir... A klog iz mir!

Worked to death oysgemutshet, oysgematert tsum toit

Worn out oysgematert

Would that it comes true! Alevei!

Very wealthy, stuffed with money ongeshtopt (slang)

Yearly remembrance of the dead yortzeit

You can go crazy! Meh ken meshugeh veren!

You can vomit from this! Meh ken brechen!

You don't frighten me! Gai strashe di gens! (Lit., go frighten the geese)

You don't have to be pretty if you are charming.   Meh darf nit zein shain, nor chainevdik.

You don't show a fool something half finished.   A nar veist men nit kain halbeh arbet.

You fool, you!   Nar ainer!

You please me a great deal.   Ir gefelt mir zaier.

You should choke on it!   Dershtikt zolstu veren!

You should get a stomach cramp!   Zol dich chapen beim boych!

You should swell up like a mountain!   Zolst geshvollen veren vi a barg!

You shouldn't know bad things!   Zolst nit vissen fun kain shlechts.

You should live (and be well)!   A laiben ahf dir!

You should live so!   Zolstu azoy laiben!

You understand?   Farshtaist?

You're all set!   Ir zeit ahfen ferd! (Lit., you're on top of the horse!)

You're not making sense.   Nisht geshtoigen un nisht gefloigen. (Lit., you're not standing and you're not flying.)

You're nuts!   Bist meshugeh! Bist tsedrait!